CARL ROGERS: DIALOGUES